Developing Leaders for Restructuring Schools

New Habits of Mind and Heart

A Report of the National LEADership Network
Study Group on Restructuring Schools

Prepared by
Charles Mojkowski, Director, Rhode Island LEAD

Edited by
Richard Bamberger, Executive Director, Capital Area
School Development Association, Albany, New York

Planning Committee
Dianne Ashby, Director, Illinois LEAD
Mary Campbell, OERI Study Group Coordinator
Richard McDonald, former Director, New York LEAD; Co-Chair
Charles Mojkowski, Director, Rhode Island LEAD; Co-Chair
Nelson Walls, Director, Maine LEAD

March 1991

U.S. Department of Education
Ted Sanders
Acting Secretary

Office of Educational Research and Improvement
Christopher T. Cross
Assistant Secretary

Programs for the Improvement of Practice
Nelson Smith
Director

March 1991

Foreword

Our Nation is committed to a course of fundamental change to improve America's educational performance. The six national goals agreed to by the President and the governors have given all of us both a vision and a challenge for making **all** of our schools centers for achievement by the end of the decade. These goals are clear, comprehensive, and oriented to results; but they are beyond attainment unless sweeping changes are made in our education system.

President Bush has noted that "when hallowed tradition proves to be hollow convention, then we must not hesitate to shatter tradition." In education, as in other areas of our national life where results fall short of expectations, progress requires a fundamental redesign. The need for such fundamental redesign is increasingly accepted and is gathering support from many quarters.

But no efforts—however enthusiastic, however thoughtful, however well-intentioned—can succeed without the inspiration and commitment of those at the heart of the education enterprise. Parents, teachers, and school administrators must lead the way and this volume reflects such leadership.

Thirty people, who are deeply involved in education, have taken the initiative to examine school restructuring and its implications. They find that great change must occur. They offer no comfortable nostrums to ease passage through the rough waters of change. Yet I, and all who read this report, must take heart from their prescription for education and school leadership. A rare blend of the heroic and mundane, of lofty ideal and pragmatic realism, it is a courageous and imaginative foray into the future.

An unusual collaboration has made this report possible. Kraft General Foods, the Department of Education, and the Institute for Educational Leadership in Washington, D.C. have worked for almost 3 years to support and extend the work of the LEAD centers in a partnership known as the National LEADership Network. With the support of a generous grant from the Kraft General Foods Foundation, this network links the 57 LEAD centers—one in each state, the District of Columbia, and six Caribbean and Pacific Island areas—in a coherent national school leadership program. The network's Study Group on Restructuring Schools is responsible for developing this volume.

I congratulate the members of the study group and other contributors to this volume and commend their work to all who will undertake the challenge of restructuring America's schools.

Christopher T. Cross
Assistant Secretary,
Office of Educational Research and Improvement
U.S. Department of Education

Preface

This report was prepared by the National LEADership Network Study Group on Restructuring Schools. The Study Group was formed at the 1988 LEAD Directors Annual Meeting to examine the implications of the emerging restructuring movement for the changing roles and training needs of administrators. Activities of the committee are supported by the National LEADership Network with funds from the Kraft General Foods Foundation.

The Study Group consists of the LEAD Directors from nine states—California, Illinois, Kansas, Kentucky, Maine, New York, Oregon, Rhode Island, and Washington—as well as representatives from two regional educational laboratories and a Study Group coordinator from the U.S. Department of Education's Office of Educational Research and Improvement (OERI).

This report addresses an important but neglected aspect of the restructuring schools movement: the education and training required for administrators of restructuring schools. Given that the restructuring process involves substantial changes in nearly every aspect of schooling, it is not surprising that the education and training requirements for administrators in these schools involve equally substantial changes, changes that we believe remain obscured by the lists of general skills provided in the popular literature on leadership. This report provides a "view from the inside," in that it is based on the experience and reflections of administrators actually involved in restructuring efforts and of LEAD Center Directors who are providing professional development services to administrators.

This report is truly a collaborative effort of all Study Group members. We sincerely appreciate their hard work and excellent contributions. We are particularly grateful to Dianne Ashby and Nelson Walls who assisted us in the coordination of the Study Group's work and to the superintendents, principals, and central office administrators listed in appendix B who shared their thoughts based on first-hand experiences with restructuring. In addition, we wish to acknowledge the assistance of the JCPS-Gheens Professional Development Academy staff, particularly Pat Todd and Terry Brooks, who hosted our study group at the Gheens Academy in April 1989, and Phillip Schlechty, President of the Center for Leadership in School Reform, who generously shared his ideas with us at that April meeting. The responsibility for this report is solely that of the Study Group, but the contributions of these colleagues are especially appreciated.

Richard McDonald
Charles Mojkowski
Co-Chairs
December 1990

Contents

Introduction

To paraphrase an observation by a noted columnist, these are typically unusual times for education. Indeed, in a decade in which events have approached the revolutionary, this time may be even more typically unusual than ever. The revolutions in our global community and economy, the impact of rapid advances in technology, and the concomitant reconceptualizations of learning and work have raised expectations for substantive change in the schools.

Calls for restructuring—reconfiguring the basic functions, operations, and organization of schools—are coming from sources in and outside of the school community. It requires that we rethink the way we go about changing and improving or, as some advocates say, not merely doing things right, but doing the right thing.

What kinds of administrators are needed to lead restructuring districts and schools? How do traditional conceptions of leadership align with school-based management and shared decision making? What skills and understandings constitute the new enlightened leadership role in a restructuring school? And how can these competencies and dispositions be nurtured in prospective and practicing administrators? These are questions our Study Group addressed.

As LEAD Center Directors responsible for designing and providing education and training for administrators, we recognize the opportunities that restructuring offers for re-examining the leadership role and its development. We understand that roles will need to change for all members of the expanded school community: teachers, school board members, parents, and those typically outside of the school community who

Restructuring requires that we rethink the way we go about changing and improving.

are keenly interested in education. Our particular focus, however, is on district and school administrators.

The press for restructuring schools can emanate from many sources inside and outside of schools. Our sense is that the most appropriate initiators and facilitators are district and school administrators. They must empower and support, and catalyze and sustain restructuring efforts. These first steps are the most critical and difficult. Administrators need help in taking them.

Three questions have guided our work:

- 1. What are the essential elements of restructuring and how are they different from traditional approaches to school improvement?

- 2. What new or expanded competencies (knowledge and understandings, skills, and attitudes) do administrators need in order to create and sustain restructuring efforts?

- 3. How should administrator development change to best enhance these new competencies?

To address these questions, we worked for over a year and a half, reviewing the research and practice literature, talking with researchers and expert practitioners, and reflecting on and analyzing our own experiences as trainers of administrators. A highlight of our work was a "select seminar" in which we joined with superintendents and principals engaged in restructuring initiatives in districts and schools throughout the

United States. This seminar helped us to expand our understanding of the day-to-day work of restructuring and to recognize the inadequacies of existing programs for preparing administrators.

The Study Group's work has enlarged our perspective and informed our judgments about the questions we addressed. From our reading, reflection, and conversations, we have arrived at the following conclusions:

- The values, beliefs, and assumptions that drive restructuring schools are very different from those of traditional schools. But these substantial differences promise to make a an actual difference in learning for students and for all members of the school community.

- Leadership matters. As schools restructure to share decision-making authority and responsibility, new forms of leadership will be essential. Administrators will need to provide that leadership in partnership with teachers.

- Restructuring involves not just schools, but the larger school community of parents, community members, and business leaders.

"Restructuring schools is a means to an end: the end being learning success for all students." [*]

---

[*] Marginal notes in quotations were taken from Select Seminar participants' personal notebooks. See appendix C for a description of the Study Group and Select Seminar processes.

The barriers are many and substantial, but they are not insurmountable. Instead, they help us appreciate the dimensions of the opportunity.

- In the spirit of Frank Lloyd Wright's principle that form follows function, the essential elements of restructuring require new administrator competencies and behaviors.

- We need to be concerned with much more than training. We need to recreate schools as learning communities where all members—teachers and administrators, as well as students—grow in and through their work.

- We need to consider new settings and processes for preparing potential and practicing administrators.

- We need new professional development structures to support administrators working in restructuring districts and schools.

- Leadership development is a shared responsibility. Institutions of higher education, professional development academies, regional labs and research centers, and the business sector must join with the schools in providing a coordinated and ongoing program of education and training.

We find the logic of these conclusions compelling. Just as schools need to restructure to better prepare all students for a rapidly changing society and economy, so also does training for administrators need to be redesigned.

In the following section of our report, we identify those aspects of restructuring we find most salient. Based on that assessment, we then describe competencies—knowledge and understandings, skills and behaviors, attitudes and dispositions—that we believe best illustrate the nature and scope of the changes that restructuring implies for new leadership roles. Following from these descriptions, we propose the essential elements of a new paradigm for providing education and training for administrators.

Restructuring schools do not create themselves; they require enlightened leadership for their initiation and sustenance. Therefore, we must attend to leadership development if we are to realize restructuring potential for improving the education of our children. The barriers are many and substantial, but they are not insurmountable. Instead, they help us to appreciate the dimensions of the opportunity restructuring presents for students and for all members of the school community.

Restructuring Schools: Changing the Way We Improve

What distinguishes restructuring schools from those undertaking more traditional approaches to improvement? Whole forests have given their lives to the hundreds of attempts to answer that question and to capture the essence of restructuring. We are not eager to contribute to the devastation, but do wish to identify those special features that have implications for school leadership and its development. We focus in this section on the differences between restructuring and traditional approaches to school improvement that we think make a difference. We also give some attention to what we consider to be essential prerequisites to restructuring. These understandings provide a foundation for the new requirements for school leadership and its development.

Rationale

To paraphrase a popular advertising slogan, restructuring is not your father's school improvement program. While it draws on much of the same knowledge base as traditional approaches, restructuring pushes back the boundaries of what these approaches take for granted. It moves beyond existing constraints through fundamental changes that are systemic in scope and strategic in approach. Such significant changes are made necessary by the magnitude of the changes taking place in the global community.

The rapidly changing global society and economy require a very different worker and citizen than the schools are now graduating. Indeed, the existing system is unable to prepare the graduates our country needs. The high percentage of dropouts, the large number of failing students

> *"Restructuring is a process, not a product. An organization (school district or school) never reaches the final state of being restructured. The process is dynamic."*

hidden behind the mean scores on standardized tests, and the graduates who are not ready for work or additional learning constitute an embarrassing testimony. Many students leave school without even minimal skills. The existing system fails as well in teaching the new basics—thinking and reasoning, problem solving, accessing and using information for knowledge production and learning—for an even larger number of students. These students will find it increasingly difficult to participate successfully and happily in our economy and society. The aim of restructuring, then, is to make needed changes in schools so that America educates all of its children for productive lives.

The accretion of small adjustments in what remains a very traditional enterprise has rendered the schools changing but unchanged. The small successes that schools realize within the existing structure often remain limited and transitory. Achieving these isolated successes by fine-tuning the existing system deludes many into believing that it's just a matter of the right reading or math program, the newest instructional technology, or a bit more emphasis on staff development. They continue to believe that, with just a few more horses and a few more men, they really can put Humpty Dumpty back together again.

However, minor adjustments will not accomplish the required transformation. The problem is structural and will not be solved by episodic and piecemeal tinkering. Fundamental flaws in the system can only be addressed by fundamental changes. To prepare the citizen and worker we want and need, the schools will have to redesign the curriculum; the teaching and learning environment; and the way in which people, time, facilities, and other resources are used to support that teaching and learning process and environment. Restructuring aims to change not only how schools operate, but the what, the why, and the way they improve.

Differences That Make a Difference

Restructuring is distinguished as much by its philosophical underpinnings as it is by its structural or operational components. Its most salient characteristics are influenced by a belief system and a vision that require radically different responses to the problems of education than are possible within current forms of schooling.

Restructuring is the process of institutionalizing essential new beliefs and values in the school mission, structure, and process. The gaps between these new essentials and the existing missions, structures, and processes signal the level and type of changes needed.

Restructuring introduces fundamental change in four key dimensions of schooling: **programs and services for students, roles and relationships, rules and regularities,** and **accountability.** Our purpose in highlighting these elements is to construct a foundation for our special task: determining what leadership competencies and behaviors are needed in order to initiate and sustain restructuring schools.

"Every day at school I uncover a new tragedy, another horror story, a further testimony that poor children are being forgotten by the rest of America, including their own communities. We are losing a generation of talented, motivated, creative children who cope tremendously well under the worst situations in their neighborhoods."

> *"Restructuring is at least as much an interior change as an exterior one: We need a better focus on what we really want to accomplish and a firmer grasp of the realities of what we can accomplish with real people and real constraints."*

Student Programs and Services

Restructuring programs and services for students requires attention to at least three major elements: student learning outcomes, the teaching and learning process and environment, and the integration of educational and social services provided to students. Restructuring, like many traditional school improvement approaches, has as one of its principal goals that all children will learn. Restructuring moves beyond that goal by calling for a reconceptualization of what all children should learn and a redesign of the teaching and learning process and environment that will achieve those outcomes. Restructuring schools do not focus on the traditional basic skills alone, but on the child who can think, learn, and perform in and across traditional subject areas. They make deliberate decisions about what they teach, establishing professional agreements about what is most important, and eliminating content in order to assure mastery of essential knowledge, skills, and values.

Restructuring schools make substantial adjustments in instructional practices, often redesigning the entire teaching and learning process and environment. In these schools, teachers

- infuse real-world learning and work into their instruction and place more responsibility on students to work both independently and collaboratively;

- use time and other resources differently to create and sustain these environments;

- provide equal and extended opportunity and access to all of the school's learning resources;

- design instructional alternatives to accommodate the range of abilities and talents; and

- reorganize instruction so that students truly understand the material presented to them (as well as the knowledge they create themselves), experience more in-depth learning as opposed to covering great amounts of content, and engage in higher-order thinking and learning tasks.

Schools are only one of several agencies that provide services to children. The number of these services and their clients is growing rapidly, particularly in large urban districts where the abundance of services threatens to asphyxiate the system. Restructuring schools attend to the whole child, coordinating school services with those of other social agencies, sometimes even providing new services that contribute to the child's overall well-being and readiness to learn.

They maintain "an eye for the whole chessboard" and recognize the interdependence and interconnectedness of educational and social services that must be used for the child's benefit.

Roles and Relationships

Restructuring schools are characterized by site autonomy, shared decision making among school staff, enhanced roles for teachers and parents, and regulatory simplicity. They redesign decision making and

Restructuring schools attend to the whole child, coordinating school services with those of other social agencies, sometimes even providing new services that contribute to the child's overall well-being and readiness to learn.

communication structures, changing roles and relationships both within the school and between the school and its external environment. The most common changes are those involving teachers, who gain increased authority and responsibility for the teaching and learning environment and for the allocation and supervision of resources including staff, time, and facilities. Most often, increased authority and responsibility are shared with the principal and district-level administrators; they are exercised through decision-making processes in which school-based teams forge agreements about improvement plans that bind individuals to a common mission. The school-based team uses shared decision-making processes to deal with decisions that matter.

Schools engaged in restructuring employ integrated top-down and bottom-up approaches to change. Organizational structures are based on networks and flexible work groups rather than hierarchies. Power, understood as the ability to achieve the mission and goals of the school, is shared among administrators and teachers in such a way that the total power of the organization is expanded.

Restructuring schools focus the attention of all professionals and the community on the student and the teaching and learning process.

Restructuring schools focus the attention of all professionals and the community on the student and the teaching and learning process. They work at creating a better match between the teaching and learning environment designed by the teachers and the organizational and management structures and procedures that are needed to support that environment. Staff, time, facilities, and other resources are allocated according to the requirements of the teaching and learning process. Restructuring attends to the principle that form follows function: the organization must accommodate the transformed ends and means of the learning process.

These schools catalyze and support new roles for teachers. They encourage risk taking and innovation. In the classroom, teachers serve as instructional designers, coaches, resources, and facilitators. Outside of the classroom, they serve as members of teams working on improvement projects agreed on by the staff. Often old roles may need to be eliminated: using teachers as bus monitors and lunchroom supervisors, for example, is inconsistent with their expanded professional responsibilities and constitutes an inefficient use of their talent and experience.

Restructuring schools attend to their organizational health, creating humanistic environments and learning communities in which all members can learn and grow. A central *modus operandi* for achieving organizational health is enhanced communication. Restructuring schools engage in a continuing conversation, focusing particularly on programs and services for children.

Schools in the process of restructuring also invest heavily in staff development that is designed by the staff and focused on the school's improvement priorities. Teacher isolation is minimized through participatory planning and development.

Such schools develop "extended families" that include parents and members of the community in responsible roles. Teachers increase their conversations with parents about learning and development. Parents take on increased responsibilities for their children's growth and develop-

"Empowerment: Stop doing for others what they can do for themselves."

ment, participate in developing new programs and services, and contribute their time to assisting teachers in facilitating learning. Restructuring schools develop an ongoing involvement with the communities they serve, attracting commitment and support for their mission and improvement priorities.

Rules and Regularities

"Education is the last of the big dinosaurs."

Because restructuring schools create organizational structures that support risk taking and innovation, they often require that external and internal controls—laws and regulations, policies and bargaining agreements—be modified or waived to allow new solutions to be tested. New rules and agreements must be constructed with the child and the teaching and learning process as the central concern. Restructuring schools focus on a mission, but deliberately maintain organizational flexibility in order to respond to new needs and opportunities.

These schools challenge the regularities of schooling—those entrenched structural and procedural conventions that typify the school organization from state to state and decade to decade. They push back the boundaries of what is taken for granted. The constants (e.g., the use of time and people) of schooling have accumulated like sediment over scores of years in response to many different external and internal pressures. Often, the regularities are anchored in past practice ("the way we've always done it"); sometimes they are written in collective bargaining agreements that constrain as much as they protect. Restructuring requires that school boards, administrators, and teachers honestly and openly renegotiate the way they will negotiate, as well as the very substance of the regularities themselves.

Schools engaged in restructuring need understanding and nurturing from district- and state-level leaders. They need enlightened policies and regulations that focus more on desired student outcomes and less on the means by which these outcomes are achieved. District- and state-level leaders need to promote risk taking and encourage innovation and variation at the school level. And they need to provide for the documentation and analysis of these variations, so that what is learned can be fed back into the ongoing process of restructuring.

Accountability

"What goes 'round, comes 'round," the saying goes. But each time around, the spin is slightly different. So it is with accountability. In restructuring schools, accountability is a central concern, but unlike previous experiences, the accountability originates as much from within the school as without. The school's accountability for all of the students is a concomitant of the school-based team's increased authority and responsibility as professionals. School boards expect accountability as before, but now gain it in exchange for providing the means to be accountable. Accountability is a function of the professional agreements established by the school-based teams. Teachers' individual autonomy is bounded by school-wide professional agreements forged by the professionals and guided by the school's vision and mission.

"It is still legitimate for a board and superintendent to have a vision for what the district and school should be— to set district expectations and goals and to expect positive results for children. Restructuring does not mean license for people in school to do their own thing."

15

Restructuring schools have their share of failures, but they fail intelligently, incorporating new knowledge into their improvement activities.

Restructuring schools use an extensive range and higher quality of information about student and organizational performance to inform their decisions about needs and priorities. They watch student performance in all essential areas, attending to real-world thinking, learning, and performing skills, as well as to the traditional basics. They attend to the appropriateness of assessment instruments and procedures that monitor students' ability to reason well and solve real-world problems, to seek and use information, and to use technology tools for increased effectiveness and productivity. They give special attention to authentic assessment, using observations, portfolios, and student performances in addition to traditional tests as means of judging progress. They place responsibility on the student for self-monitoring and assessment. These schools exhibit an increased openness to information, incorporating interactive testing and adjustment into their risk taking and innovation. Restructuring schools have their share of failures, but they fail intelligently, incorporating new knowledge into their future improvement activities.

No One Best Model

While there is substantial consensus on the rationale and key elements of restructuring, there is no fixed recipe, no one sure formula for success. The vision and values that guide it can be realized in many ways, according to local needs, resources, and traditions. Moreover, each constituent group emphasizes different features of restructuring. Teachers, for example, give special significance to their increased authority and responsibility. Principals and superintendents particularly applaud the decrease in external regulations that constrain the way they allocate and manage resources. School boards attend particularly to the increased accountability for essential learning outcomes. Parents respond positively to the child-centered decision making that promotes a holistic view of each student. The business community applauds the increased attention to creating real-world learning and work environments and performance assessments.

Restructuring Up Close

Restructurers say that the biggest challenges they face include running the existing enterprise at full tilt, while creating and introducing a new one. They must find time for the million-and-one new demands restructuring creates, recognizing and rewarding the exceptional efforts of committed and overworked staff, and hurdling the obstacles that trip them up at every innovative step. In addition, they need to find occasions for professional contact with peers who share their frustrations and fears, confirm the worth of their efforts, and offer possible solutions for intractable problems. There are no blueprints for this undertaking, no packaged programs or ready answers. Educators in the middle of the restructuring maelstrom say they have learned not to depend on canned wisdom but to "lead with our hearts."

Certain principles and characteristics seem to define their experience.

Risk Taking. Restructuring schools foster climates that encourage and support risk-taking behavior. Ample evidence indicates that school staff tend to take a conservative approach to the job. Tradition and con-

"Sometimes we (principals) feel like the parachutist who has taken the jump with our troops only to be disappointed to find a scarcity of supplies, tools, and support to accomplish the mission after we land."

vention hold powerful sway in education. But the demands placed on schools today call for greater independence of action, bolder imagination and, ultimately, greater discretion and professional growth for both building-level administrators and teachers. Through taking informed risks, they achieve both innovation and professional development.

Communication. Traditional schools constrain communication to hierarchical, formal channels. Teachers work autonomously, isolated in their classrooms. Administrators and teachers confer over administrative or bureaucratic matters, but too infrequently about instructional revitalization. Administrators rarely communicate with peers in other buildings or districts. There is much paper work and even much personal interaction, but communication is scarce. Restructuring, however, places a premium on communication. Novel allocations of time, space, funds, and authority create the need for vast amounts of information and frequent human contact—to supply new facts and ideas, to penetrate confusion and uncertainty, and to promote new forms of working together.

Collaboration. Restructuring is a collaborative process. Collaboration takes place among teachers planning instruction, among administrators and teachers designing new programs, and among building administrators or leadership teams and central office staff developing a mission and goals. Individual autonomy—and the comforts that go with it—yields to collegiality and shared responsibility and the risks and efforts they entail.

Local Innovation. The educational quality envisioned for restructuring schools requires variation, responsiveness, experimentation—in

"Shared decision making is not a solution. It is a process to arrive at a solution."

short, innovation—at the building level. There are many ways of arriving at the goals of restructuring, but none can be explicitly predetermined and what works at any one moment may only do so because of some unique and unspecified preceding condition. When imagination and daring are united in organized innovation at the building level and are supported by the district, they provide the needed day-to-day stimulus to deal with unforeseen challenges.

Professional Accountability. Individual discretion and organizational control wage a constant battle in most bureaucratic institutions. The more hierarchical and conservative the institution, the greater the emphasis on control over discretion. Restructuring calls for the richest amount of individual discretion consistent with responsiveness to community and professional mandates. Professional accountability encourages the wise use of discretion by 1) holding educators accountable for the correctness of their decisions and judgments, rather than solely for results; 2) holding the collective school team accountable for the results attributable, not to any one individual, but to the whole education team; and 3) applying standards of success that accurately measure desired outcomes and provide constructive information for improvement.

Professionalization. Restructuring ensures that the best quality teaching is provided by a truly professional teacher workforce, in which clear and correct standards of mastery govern entry into the profession; teachers exercise responsibility for curriculum and instruction and are accountable for the correctness of their decisions; and working conditions encourage and reward professional conduct. Where teachers and admin-

"If we believe that all kids can learn, we should act as if all members of the organization can learn also."

istrators collaborate in instructional decision making and norms of collegiality guide staff interaction, resources will be best allocated, morale will be high, and instruction will be competent.

Rejection of conventional stereotypes. The demands of our democratic society and the larger geopolitical system require that we acknowledge, accept, and build on the many expressions of intelligence that prompt excellence of many kinds. We must promote the competence of women in "a man's world" and the contributions of the earliest as well as the most recent Americans to our society and culture. School processes freed of stereotypes and appreciative of rich variation and potential among individuals demand much from teachers and administrators, but their acceptance rewards society with inestimable resources.

Flexibility and resilience. Restructuring schools demonstrate flexibility in yielding to new pressures and imperatives. Guided by shared beliefs and values and informed by others' experience and their own, they are able to learn and adjust. Restructuring requires that schools discard old skins, much like the crab that throws off the too-tight skeleton that constrains further growth. The old shell cannot accommodate the new form. In restructuring schools, administrators and teachers discard unproductive behaviors, unlearn obsolete skills, and cultivate new values and dispositions. Discarding unproductive and inhibiting behaviors and attitudes can contribute as much to restructuring as acquiring facilitating ones. Often staff must throw off old behaviors and dispositions before new ones are fully formed. During this "molting period," restructuring schools are vulnerable, waiting for the new structure to strengthen sufficiently to accommodate the new mission and context.

> *"Discarding unproductive and inhibiting behaviors and attitudes can contribute as much to restructuring as acquiring facilitating ones."*

A Word About Prerequisites

Restructuring schools do not spring into existence spontaneously. Their emergence is a product of many diverse and complex forces and conditions. In our study of restructuring schools, we identified several conditions that may be considered prerequisites to initiating the process.

Readiness to change. Restructuring efforts typically grow out of a dissatisfaction with existing conditions and a frustration with the existing organization. Without sufficient and widespread dissatisfaction and frustration, there may not be a disposition to try radically different approaches to improvement. Successful change must be fueled by real commitment.

Incentives. Substantial frustration with the status quo may not be sufficient to encourage restructuring unless state and district leaders provide incentives to do things differently. Incentives are most often positive inducements, but can be negatives. Positive incentives include encouragement (from school boards, superintendents, and the community) to take risks, time for planning, and additional resources. Negative incentives can be mandates and general or specific expressions of dissatisfaction. Research and experience indicate that an opportunity to participate as professionals on important work is a very powerful incentive for teachers and administrators.

Positive working conditions. Often restructuring cannot take place unless basic working conditions are positive. These conditions include security and an atmosphere of trust and mutual respect, as well as the

"The current formal rewards (salary and economic) and informal incentives (assignment, status) may not be consistent with restructuring schools. How do we change them, given the tremendous forces that maintain the status quo (single salary schedule and sharp divisions between administrative and teacher responsibility)?"

more traditional needs for sufficient time and other resources to adequately accomplish the task.

Resources. The most valuable of resources is time for teachers and administrators to work together on improvement tasks. Often money is needed to compensate teachers, procure substitutes, or obtain other resources for initiating the restructuring process.

Skilled leadership. An important prerequisite is enlightened leadership. Without such leadership at the district and school levels, teachers are unlikely to confer the entitlement to initiate the change process. The skills to provide "lift-off power" as well as sustained support to a school or district are neither common nor easily developed. Insightful and sensitive leadership is a central catalyst.

Restructuring schools aim for the achievement of a new set of education values. They are inspired by a new mission and vision of what is possible—of what is imperative—in American education and by the determination to invent new ways to achieve it. There is no one right way for schools to restructure, but we consider these elements—reinvigorated programs and services, expanded roles and responsibilities, reconstituted rules and regularities, and reconceptualized accountability—to be the common, salient elements distinguishing restructuring schools from incrementally improving schools.

Change of this magnitude calls not only for administrators who are expert in the research knowledge and technical skills of restructuring, but

"There is great pressure to demonstrate results quickly. If restructuring is ongoing and if fundamental systemic change is to occur, time will be needed to demonstrate results. We want more than tinkering. How do we convince the public to give the schools some time?"

also for educators who have learned to "lead with their hearts." We describe this enlightened leader in the following section.

Reinventing the Leadership Role

Initiating and sustaining restructuring schools calls for new kinds of leadership knowledge, skills, and attitudes and a capacity for combining them in innovative ways. Restructuring efforts are by their nature "bootstrapped" endeavors, relying on the existing system of people and resources to renew themselves. Restructurers ask where they can stand to leverage the system. We believe the leveraging point is the school administrator.

But to leverage the existing system and initiate and sustain restructuring schools, administrators will need to reconceive their leadership role and to value the use of new and enhanced competencies.

We propose that leaders of restructuring schools do things differently than do traditional leaders and redesign their leadership behaviors to correspond to a different world view about learning, schools, and leading. To support our argument, we look beyond the lists of leadership competencies promulgated in the popular and research literature. For we believe that the circumstances of restructuring—the very logic of restructuring—call for a new conceptualization of the leadership role, as well as an appreciation of the many decisions and actions that consume the day of a leader in a restructuring school.

New Habits of Mind and Heart

Einstein was once asked how it was that he came to his discovery of relativity. He answered, "It was easy; all I had to do was ignore an axiom." The transformation of school leadership and leaders for restructuring schools also may require that we ignore a few axioms.

> **Restructuring efforts are by their nature "bootstrapped" endeavors, relying on the existing system of people and resources to renew themselves.**

> *"Principals' roles must change—to that of coach and facilitator, not manager of buildings and status quo."*

In moving from our views of restructuring to implications for educating and training school leaders, we examine a few "non-axiomatic" behaviors that illustrate the way the leadership role needs to be reinvented. We put aside from the outset the common and all too numerous lists of leadership skills and behaviors. Our intent is not to deny the importance of the existing taxonomies of leadership skills or to diminish the utility of the portraits of skillful leaders they depict. We wish, though, to reach a deeper understanding of leadership skills and to capture the essence of the real-world, day-to-day behaviors that superintendents, principals, and other leaders must exhibit in order to catalyze and maintain restructuring environments.

What is often lost in the taxonomies is the whole that is greater than the sum of its parts, the sense of the real-world, day-to-day action most characteristic of principals, superintendents, and others who catalyze and sustain restructuring environments. In this section, we try to portray the overall character of such leadership and the subtleties and dynamics that differentiate between leadership new and old.

If a factory-model school calls for a foreman or plant manager, what do restructuring schools call for? The restructuring leader is at the nexus of community changes, child and adult development, and academic programming; and, as such, perhaps no one label can adequately describe the administrator's responsibility. We believe that the overall role calls for a persuasive and systematic concentration of one's own and others' efforts, in combination with essential resources, to engage the organization in a process of developing and implementing increasingly sophisticated, worthy educational values and outcomes.

Leaders of restructuring schools, in our view, take on the challenge of developing new student programs and services, roles and relationships, rules and regularities, and accountability to fulfill new visions of what is possible for children and for schools. Such basic changes require much of these committed leaders—that they come endowed with strong values and a well defined worldview and strong principles capable of guiding the growth of new values and perspectives; that they be willing to set aside control for enablement; that they rely less on technical skills and more on personal qualities needed to inspire and maintain concentrated human effort; that they give greater emphasis to crafting suitable problems and goals than to implementing formulaic solutions to textbook problems; and that they commit themselves and others to an uncertain, iterative process while resisting the temptation to assent to a known and predictable, but lesser, future.

The ends of restructuring are not necessarily given, nor are the means always evident. The discovery of suitable ends and the application of appropriate means are often simultaneous puzzles the restructuring leader solves in collaboration with colleagues and community. So the identification and adoption of guiding values, often within a context of considerable ambiguity and conflict, is the leader's first task.

Restructuring calls for powerful personal and technical skills; but most important are the character and the will to support others daily as they take on major challenges and see them through to the end. The situations of restructuring can rarely be precisely defined and made to fit a blueprint. The leader will rarely have the luxury of unambiguous analysis and prescription of skills to fit the task. As our colleagues in restructuring systems have told us, "We must lead with our hearts as often as we follow our plans."

Leaders of restructuring schools

Create dissonance. Using a variety of methods, new leaders constantly remind staff and others of the gap between the vision that they have for their children and their current actions and accomplishments. They use this dissonance to create a press for improvement.

Prepare for and create opportunities. They exhibit a constructive and creative opportunism. They pursue opportunities that will move the school closer to the accomplishment of its mission and ignore those that do not.

Forge connections and create interdependencies. They create new roles and relationships. They dismantle the egg-crate structure of schools and create opportunities and processes to connect teachers within and across disciplines and to connect people inside and outside of the school community to one another. By skillfully creating interdependencies, leaders create the consensus for understanding and action that is required in restructuring environments. The analogy to an orchestra leader is often employed to describe the subtle ways in which these leaders bind independent entrepreneurs to a shared vision and mission.

Encourage risk taking. School people typically are uncomfortable with taking risks. Premature and arbitrary judgments too often inhibit

"The thrill of leading a school must come through success rather than power."

creativity and risk taking. Leaders of restructuring schools create environments and conditions that provide increased comfort with making mistakes and learning from them. These leaders protect risk takers from premature judgments of failure.

Follow as well as lead. Leaders recreate themselves throughout the organization, nurturing leadership behaviors in all staff. They lead through service rather than position, providing support and good "follow-ship" to ad hoc leaders.

Use information. Administrators in restructuring environments use a wide variety of information about student and organizational performance. They are clear communicators who use multiple channels for accessing and distributing information. They create new ways to think about and measure the growth and productivity of learners and the learning process. Leaders use research and practice information to guide innovation and change. They monitor and document the implementation process.

Foster the long view. Impatience is a prominent American virtue with serious side effects. Leaders know when and how to delay judgment, tolerate and learn from interim setbacks, and invest for long-term yields. They know "when to hold them and when to fold them," guided by their sense of mission and strategic direction. They work incrementally within a comprehensive design of restructuring, guided by their vision of learners and learning. The special requirements of restructuring—moving incrementally within a comprehensive design—require a highly skilled leader and facilitator.

"It really is not difficult to identify the skills needed by principals who are to lead restructuring efforts. The challenge is to assess candidates for the principalship for their level of such skills and to develop training experiences to assist them in developing and expanding such skills."

Acquire resources. They are particularly adept at resource acquisition and distribution and finding flexible resources through competitive grants and assistance from businesses and community organizations. They practice resource reallocation and cost containment. They have a simultaneous macro- and micro-orientation, identifying pockets of readiness and resistance and allocating resources accordingly. They find time for staff to plan and develop.

Negotiate for win-win outcomes. They work constructively and creatively with teacher representatives within the collective bargaining agreement. They use the collective bargaining process to forge new professional agreements dealing with the teaching and learning process.

Employ change strategies. The research on change management contains ample tools for analysis and intervention. Leaders are skilled in analyzing concerns and levels of commitment. They configure the right mix of strategies and tactics to keep new undertakings on track through all stages of an improvement effort. These leaders are change strategists, recognizing the dynamics of their organization and determining the potential for change.

Provide stability in change. The elimination function (the deliberate abandonment of elements of the organization that have not worked previously) needs to be accompanied by a framework that provides stability while the changes are taking place. Restructuring leaders construct a scaffolding for the organization and its people so that they can experiment with new ideas, take risks, and dismantle some aspects of the organization without losing a sense of the overall framework in which they are

"Look at what is not working and see it as a possibility."

working. These leaders provide order and direction in an ambiguous and uncertain environment.

Grow people while getting the work accomplished. Formal staff development is only one means of developing staff and others in the school community. Often the most powerful learning is accomplished while meaningful work is being done. Leaders help staff to move, in their thinking and behavior, beyond the limits of their own experience. They create self-managing and self-learning groups and invest heavily in staff development. They identify and nurture potential leaders to ensure that the foundation for restructuring will endure beyond their tenure.

New Wine, New Skins

Clearly, leaders of restructuring schools do not work within the confines of a well-defined, clearly-circumscribed role. In fact, the concept of role may be inappropriate for a job of this sort. For "role" implies a patterned set of behaviors constructed to suit defined situations in organizations or social systems. It suggests regularity, predictability, and routinization. Hallmarks of bureaucratic organizations, these dimensions are anathema to restructuring schools.

Instead of *role*, we should perhaps be concerned with something on the order of *character*. It defines the whole person and the full measure of the professional undertaking, without the infirmities of listed qualities that miss the essence of the whole. Like other human endeavors that escape precise measurement—parenting, artistic performance, or generalship—leadership of the sort needed for restructuring schools is best

"Leaders help staff to move, in their thinking and behavior, beyond the limits of their own experience."

31

defined by a set of gyroscopic forces through which the improving school and its changing environment are kept in harmony.

Clearly, leaders in restructuring schools are radically different from their counterparts in traditional schools. They spend their time differently, allocating extra time to enhancing the health of the organization and focusing on people inside and outside the school who can help to achieve its mission and goals. Intent on continuous improvement, these leaders share authority and responsibility in order to multiply the power of the organization to decide upon and achieve its goals. Sure of purpose but uncertain about plans, they engage others in exercises of faith as well as technique, of human development as well as attention to operational detail.

Restructuring antiquates skills used to control and celebrates capacities for trust, discretion, and responsibility. A *clear sense of purpose* must guide the leader of the restructuring enterprise. With that as a lodestar, correct action can be discerned by the logic of the compelling direction ahead.

Empowerment of others means not to abandon the responsibilities of leadership, but to *fix in others, on whom the job rests, both the sense of direction and the responsibility for its achievement*. Since no leader can compel or control effective action of subordinates in such circumstances, what must be done is to locate the impetus for effective performance in the people who must do the work.

Teachers and others who engage in social services use the term "co-production" to describe processes of teaching and learning and other service-oriented undertakings in which both parties must cooperate to achieve a common end. Unilateral action and attempts to control the process by either party are ineffective.

So it is with leadership and decision making in restructuring schools. The daily tasks of leadership and decision making must be informed by a *deep commitment to collaborative action and shared decision making*.

Wise choices in education are determined largely by context. Research demonstrates that effective teaching techniques depend upon the subject matter and that cognitive processes depend upon the field of knowledge. There is hardly any decision on which a school staff collaborates that should not be informed by a *thorough knowledge of the content area and pedagogical consequences* of one choice or another. We do not expect that every administrator will be as well versed in all subject matter as the school's teachers. But leaders must know the basics of the subjects and disciplines and must appreciate the techniques of effective teaching. They must keep abreast of developments in academic knowledge and pedagogy; they must be skilled assessors of ability and coaches of skilled development.

Leaders must be especially competent as coaches and cheerleaders. Some may find these images juvenile or not sufficiently serious. We think they express the essence of mentoring at the heart of mastery in any field, from violin, to physics, to figure skating. Once again, administrators use

The daily tasks of leadership and decision making must be informed by a deep commitment to collaborative action and shared decision making.

Mentoring [is] at the heart of mastery in any field.

these words to describe what they find to be among their most important functions, especially in the early going. Teaching ability must be developed by the maturing teacher; it is not handed over by experts, caught, or implanted. But development of any such complex and formidable skill comes from *guided experimentation, example, reflection informed by expert insight, and structure choices that inspire one to stretch beyond what one knows now to be possible.*

It is a paradox of restructuring that participants are uncertain about what they and others are doing while, at the same time, they are firmly committed to explanations for events around them that conflict with explanations held equally strongly by others. *Shared uncertainty and certain conflict can only be mitigated through communication—constant, interactive, unfettered, pervasive, and redundant communication.* Communication is valuable not only for its face content, but also as an exercise in fixing meaning, exploring the boundaries of shared values, testing for readiness and obstacles, and raising explicitly implicit ideas and concerns. There must be constant opportunity to test perceptions, to ease doubts, to air and perhaps resolve contradictions, to gain reassurance, to quell rumor and share hopes, and to confirm through human contact that participants are engaged in a formidable but wonderful task.

Restructuring calls for:

Courage, faith, and persistence. This means the courage to act on conviction in the face of uncertainty or doubt; the faith to act on what is right though not proven and to attract others to rightminded views; and the persistence to see through to the end a worthy undertaking. In his poem, *The Abnormal Is Not Courage,* the American poet Jack Gilbert writes in praise of "the normal excellence of long accomplishment." We, too, believe that most courage comes in the accumulation of small steps into the future sustained over time. Fear and comfort are as compelling in small doses as large, and the small efforts to resist them are as heroic as those of the Olympians.

Openness, experimentation, flexibility, resilience. Change brings the predictable as well as the unexpected. What is new is predictably resisted and derided. Careful planning falls victim to unforeseen obstacles as well as to opportunity. Both the predictable and the unexpected call for even-handed, patient persistence as well as willingness to strike while the iron is hot, to seize opportunity, or take skeptics by surprise. Close-minded or inflexible approaches fail at both. *Those who are prepared for the challenges of the predictable and unexpected find reserves of openness, experimentation, flexibility, and resilience.* They can bear and do far more than they thought possible.

Values of maturity and experience. Successful restructurers take their lot seriously but not personally. That is, they are objective about events, their meaning, and their consequences. Though deeply committed to the course of their and others' efforts, their sense of their own and of others' self and worth is not bound up in the swirl of events around them. *Free from selfish or distorted impressions, they can make judgments and take action in the best interests of the task at hand.* Such maturity comes from depth and keenness of experience, whether direct or vicarious. Some corners of life must be peered into with one's own eyes; others can be appreciated through the knowledgeable reports of others. *Opportunities to make* *responsible choices and bear their consequences, mentoring from wiser and es-teemed superiors, wide reading in the humanities as well as the social sciences, abundant conversation, persistent and honest reflection, and the selfconscious de-velopment of a repertoire of life situations and possible responses all constitute the essential experiences* that lead to maturity.

Reflection and judgment. There are points in every restructuring effort where one must rely entirely upon one's own resources, when textbook problems, prearranged criteria, and leadership formulas stand by, useless and irrelevant. Eventually, the deepest knowledge springs from reflection, and judgment feeds the truest decisions. The former Secretary of State, Dean Acheson, is said to have instructed his subordinates, "When in doubt, do the right thing." In time of doubt, practiced reflection and judgment enable the restructuring leader to "do the right thing."

What enables them to accomplish these labors, and how should we seek to differentiate their qualities from those of the traditional school leader? In many respects, the effective leader of a restructuring school is no different from the effective leader anywhere. We have grown accustomed, however, to defining leadership in education in terms of managerial and essentially conformist bureaucratic terms. In the next section, we turn to the elements of preparation.

Before Moving On ...

Because of our focus on restructuring schools, most of our remarks target building principals and teachers and the development of new forms of school-based leadership. We recognize, however, that the success of restructuring efforts is highly dependent on the commitments of the superintendent and the school board, and that their leadership behaviors will need to change as well. The impetus and support of the district superintendent are critical; the permission and incentives provided by the school board are essential. But the day-to-day leadership behaviors of the building principal are the lifeblood of restructuring schools.

If these competencies constitute a transformed syllabus for leadership development, then we must look closely at the system of education and training that will help us prepare these leaders and to advance the mission of restructuring.

The impetus and support of the district superintendent are critical; the permission and incentives provided by the school board are essential.

Restructuring Leadership Development

The transformed role for leaders of restructuring schools requires a similarly transformed program for leadership development. In this section, we suggest ways of moving beyond traditional conceptualizations of preservice and inservice programs to create the kinds of learning environments and processes that are required for preparing and supporting restructuring leaders. We propose that the responsibilities for designing and providing this education and training be shared among the many stakeholders in the education and training field.

Our deliberations and recommendations on educating and training administrators for restructuring schools are set within the broader context of professional development. This area has benefited from a resurgence of interest, funding, and new knowledge in recent years. With these resources, the wherewithal to design effective staff development programs has increased dramatically, and we build on this foundation in proposing designs for educating and training the leaders of our restructuring schools.

In brief, we premise our specific recommendations on the foundation of knowledge contained in 1) the general literature on staff development deriving from theories of adult learning and development, institutional change, and implementation research; and 2) the body of developing knowledge known to some as the "new inservice" and innovative preparation programs for the aspiring administrator.

Built upon these improvements in administrator education and training programs, we believe additional changes are needed in three areas: the **syllabus**, the **setting**, and the **process**. We view these changes as

We believe additional changes are needed in three areas: the syllabus, the setting, and the process.

39

a set of design requirements for preparing leaders of restructuring schools.

The following principles apply:

1. Programs must be based upon the state of the art in adult staff development programs.

2. The syllabus must present a coherent developmental program tailored to the functions and competencies called for in leading restructuring schools.

3. The setting must provide real and important occasions for the exercise and development of competence in restructuring.

4. Processes which themselves embody the principles of restructuring must be employed.

Creating a Learning Environment

Syllabus

The training syllabus for restructuring must focus on more than a set of topics and skills organized into modules. It must organize the behaviors and competencies that are essential to the four basic elements of restructuring schools (programs and services, roles and relationships, rules and regularities, and accountability) into a coherent development program.

The syllabus needs to blend attention to technical skills, such as resource acquisition and management and information use, with a heavier concentration on people management skills, such as creating dissonance, encouraging risk taking, and forging interdependencies. Training administrators for restructuring programs must prepare them to unleash and direct their powerful people resources toward the mission, goals, and improvement priorities of the schools. The emphasis on people management skills is a principal characteristic of education and training in and for restructuring schools.

The syllabus must draw as well on the growing body of theoretical and research information, supporting trainees in making connections between principles and practice. Leaders must learn how to keep abreast of relevant research and practice information and integrate it into their work.

How is this to be done?

Much of what the successful restructurer must have at his or her command is not specific skills to restructure or to accomplish the separate tasks of restructuring, but a broad base of knowledge and keen appreciation for the human and organizational issues and dynamics at the heart of the process. There probably is no single, isolated skill called "risk taking" or "enablement." These are practices that grow out of a base of knowledge and an appreciation for the complex interplay of academic knowledge, historical analysis and experience, insight into human character and behavior, perceptions of interesting and pertinent patterns, and the capacity and persistence to transform vision into practice.

We seek, therefore, a syllabus that teaches not skills, *per se*, but foundation knowledge that enables the leader to formulate correct action in the face of situations the leader defines.

We seek, therefore, a syllabus that teaches not skills, *per se*, but the foundation knowledge that enables the leader to formulate correct action in the face of situations the leader defines. Where the so-called situational leadership model prescribes given styles or skills for given situations, we suggest there can be no such one-to-one correspondence, nor can situations or styles be prescribed. Instead, out of the myriad possibilities within an organization's stream of experience, the leader defines the situation and produces the appropriate response to it as a single act borne of experience, knowledge, insight, and confidence. When a leadership act is accomplished, its rightness is often determined by the leader's efforts to encourage interpretations by the organization that make it right. When it is not right, or not quite right, it has produced the occasion for new learning that can then be brought to bear in making another, more appropriate choice.

The syllabus that prepares the school leader for such responsibilities should contain the following elements:

Content knowledge. Knowledge of the content of the curriculum is essential. Every leader in education must have mastered the core curriculum. Moreover, the leader's mastery must extend in sophistication and grasp well beyond that expected of the students.

Pedagogical knowledge. Leaders of restructuring schools need not be expert teachers. They must be expert coaches of teachers, however, and their knowledge of pedagogy must be sound enough to inform wise decisions in the allocation and supervision of time, space, instruction, and assessment.

Theory of education and schooling. Restructuring is a value- and theory-driven process. It springs from dissatisfaction with schooling as it is, and a rejection of conventional values and beliefs. It is guided by a sure vision of what schooling can be and what the aims of education are. *Horace's Compromise*, the path-breaking manifesto by Theodore Sizer, is one exemplar of such vision.

Social and institutional processes. Schools are at the center of a vortex of social processes, including political, economic, and demographic forces. Restructuring leaders must understand these forces and know how to work with them. At the level of the individual school, leaders must be well versed in the theory and practice of organizational dynamics, industrial psychology, institutional change, and decision making.

Collaborative work skills. We mean by collaborative work skills the set of attitudes and understandings that enable the leader to work effectively with diverse work groups, to draw from staff and community the best they have to offer, to use cooperation and conflict to advantage, to organize and direct disparate efforts into productive output, and to inspire and unite fragmented elements of any population behind a common vision.

Effective work within a context of ambiguity. Most management skills—planning, evaluation, decision analysis, staff development—of the

Leaders of restructuring schools must be expert coaches of teachers.

past three decades have been based on rational assumptions about human and organizational behavior. Schools and their inhabitants function only in part on rational grounds, however; they work like most complex social units, in unclear, ambiguous ways. Ambiguity need not mean lack of productivity, but rational methods used in ambiguous circumstances often waste efforts and create frustration. An ample foundation exists in decision theory and the social psychology of organizing to provide needed training in this area.

Exposure to the humanities. The humanities capture the depths of the human condition in ways that lie beyond the reach of the physical or social sciences. They are essential to the development not of mastery of specific knowledge, but a disciplined and empathic appreciation of what it is to be human and to meet that condition effectively.

Habits of mind and of the heart. Preparation for administrative leadership is but the start of an ongoing pursuit of skillful practice. Demands of the job and the times will change in the course of a career, as will each individual practitioner. The early training must provide, or reinforce, a lifelong commitment to certain habits of mind and of the heart that engage the leader in continuous development of intellect and character: keen interest and curiosity in the world around; effort to stay abreast of the subject and pedagogical content of one's teaching colleagues; development as, what Donald Schön calls, a "reflective practitioner"; lively reading, writing, and conversation; and cultivation of the individual and communitarian virtues of Western society.

The early training must provide, or reinforce, a lifelong commitment to certain habits of mind and of the heart that engage the leader in continuous development of intellect and character.

44

Setting

We believe the most appropriate settings for developing leaders are within schools that are restructuring or planning to restructure. Such contexts provide a fertile environment for blending theory with practice and for forming a learning community within the school. While cogent arguments can be made for conducting inservice training off-campus for an extended period of study and reflection, we are wary of programs that remove the developing leader from the restructuring context. Providers of training need to build opportunities for study and reflection into the restructuring site. They need to provide a better balance between off-campus and on-site learning and work.

Restructuring schools value learning rather than control and encourage the risk taking that serves as the foundation for new learning. Staff development itself needs to be more broadly conceptualized as an enabling environment, a learning community in which all members grow and develop. A restructuring environment is focused on problem finding and problem solving as ongoing and iterative learning processes, not a technical process of solution finding, but an organic process of learning and growing.

Such a setting also allows for what has been characterized as "succession leadership," the professional development of teachers as potential administrators. By participating in training, as well as sharing decision-making responsibilities, teachers can practice leadership behaviors and administrators can identify and nurture these potential leaders.

We believe the most appropriate settings for developing leaders ... are schools that are restructuring or planning to restructure.

We are equally convinced that a considerable portion of preservice training needs to be accomplished at the school site.

We are equally convinced that a considerable portion of preservice training needs to be accomplished at the school site. We agree with the thrust of the report of the National Commission on Excellence in Educational Administration calling for field-based programs and partnerships between universities and school districts.

The National Policy Board on Educational Administration has strongly recommended that preservice programs be primarily on-campus and cohort-based. While we understand their logic and support their aim of dramatic improvements in the quality of both programs and graduates, we believe there is far more room for alternative programs. Where cohorts are possible and where on-campus programs can be made compatible with substantial field-based internships, we endorse the notion. Otherwise, however, we believe that substantive, quality, effective programs can be provided through carefully designed and mentored individual job-centered study.

Important advances in preparation and development (primarily preservice, but we think also inservice) have been made in areas called "organizational setting" and "follow through." Pioneered by the California School Leadership Academy, these are supplementary program activities that strengthen the transference of training effects to the implementation site. These efforts provide the host site and training supervisors with complementary training, and provide post-training exercises at the job site to reinforce and extend the initial training outcomes. Where training is provided away from the work site, concern for organizational setting and follow through must be built into the training design. Where training is provided on site, these dimensions can be built into the program by team participation, organizing training around real problems and their resolution, and structured peer and mentoring relationships.

Principals, superintendents, community members, teachers—anyone deeply engaged in the challenges of restructuring—have said to us over and over: "Perhaps the most important thing we can do is to meet with our peers. We are isolated. We draw great strength and find such rich ideas from our contact with peers. But we haven't the opportunity to do nearly enough of it." Whether within a single district, an entire state, or the breadth of the Nation, practitioners of restructuring are isolated and desperately in need of peer support and learning. The LEAD Program, inspired by the New York LEAD Center, has pioneered the development of the "select seminar," a process for capturing the craft wisdom of practicing educators and sharing it among participants. Other LEAD centers and several state administrator associations have established electronic networks that enable administrators to communicate directly and conveniently with one another. Whether through select seminars, electronic networks, or conventional conferences, restructuring administrators need opportunities for frank and supportive peer interaction.

We need a comprehensive approach to creating an ongoing learning environment for all members of the organization. Just as restructuring schools create learning environments for students which integrate learning and work, they must do the same for their professionals. Such systems may require that administrators extend and reorganize the school day and year for professionals.

> *"One quickly becomes a veteran in this process ... There is a need for a 'network of veterans'."*

Process

We believe that the education and training process should 1) integrate learning and work; 2) emphasize action-oriented, problem-solving approaches to training; 3) focus on the development of teams; and 4) be comprehensive, coherent, and continuous.

While the process must be based on sound principles of adult learning and development, it may be necessary to ignore a few axioms. The process must be based on the considerable body of sound staff development that already exists and, then, it must go beyond what is now available in key respects. Even the state-of-the-art knowledge is nowhere near the standard of practice at the moment. The first task of developing training suitable for the needs of restructuring leaders is to bring what is presently being offered into conformance with the acknowledged principles of sound adult learning and development, of policy implementation, and of institutional change. The second task is to integrate staff development into the routine practices of restructuring schools.

By arguing for a change of venue to the school site, we hope to influence or change the way in which the training is provided. We do not suggest that the change is as simplistic as conducting training in an empty classroom after the end of the school day. Instead, we propose to make training an integral part of the routine operation of restructuring schools. It is important that staff development be seen not as something special and different, something external, contrived, and appended to the real work of the school. So often in our schools we seem to be saying, "work is work, and learning is learning," as though the two were incompatible. As

It may be necessary to ignore a few axioms.

part of the reorganization and reallocation of school resources, staff development should become one of the several activities or dimensions of school activity in which teachers and administrators regularly engage.

The training should reflect the work of the school and incorporate problem-centered training materials. Case studies of restructuring leaders and environments are essential. We need to translate the taxonomies of new leadership skills and behaviors into powerful learning episodes that are securely rooted in restructuring experiences. Portfolios, performances, simulations, and reflective writing will support a problem-centered orientation.

Part of our overall strategy for preparing leaders for restructuring schools is to grow from within, to identify teachers who are potential leaders, to involve them over time in increasing amounts of responsibility for restructuring situations, invest in their development while they are teachers, and give them increasing responsibilities for leadership tasks. Some training will need to be focused exclusively on administrators, but a substantial portion of the training might be more appropriately provided to administrator/teacher teams.

The restructuring school requires a broad and continuing education and training program for all members of the school community. The interdependencies that are a deliberate creation of restructuring schools require an integrated development program. School board members, central office staff, and other key individuals should participate in the training program. The American Association of School Administrators has developed just such a training design called Instructional Impact

Some training will need to be focused exclusively on administrators, but a substantial portion might be more appropriately provided to administrator/teacher teams.

Teams in which a vertically integrated team—a school board representative, superintendent, building administrators, and teachers—work and train together to introduce and master effective instruction.

Training for restructuring must be ongoing. This requirement is at odds with most present practice, which focuses on one-shot training episodes. The skills required of restructuring administrators are not amenable to a single-day workshop or even a year-long effort. The "Whitman Sampler" approach to leadership training will not do, just as addressing a simple taxonomy of leadership skills does not adequately describe the school leaders needed for restructuring schools.

Every administrator must have a personal development plan, and every school must have a coherent staff development plan in which the individual's career and the school development are viewed as organic entities extending seamlessly over time.

No one can deny that school facilities planning, school law, and other subjects around which millions of dollars (as well as careers) flow have a place in preparation and development programs. How prominently they should figure, at what point in an extended program of training they should be introduced, and how deeply participants should be exposed to them are vexing questions. Building administration is unlike almost any other profession in that the new administrator may well acquire the entire responsibility for the school in one stroke without prior experience. To this dilemma, we offer no firm solutions but some initial notions.

"The 'Whitman Sampler' approach to leadership training will not do."

Restructuring should entail changes in central offices as well as school buildings. District staff need to stress facilitation and enablement and de-emphasize control and compliance. Central offices might retain small troubleshooting staffs, competent in the specialties of plant management, personnel and bargaining, law, transportation, and other technical subjects, who would be detailed to work in trouble spots with administrators in charge. Field administrators might rotate on occasion into these slots, where they would develop and use expertise in the subject matter as well as in facilitation of problems of site administrators.

Teachers are understandably reluctant to become burdened with administrative chores. Yet restructuring schools will require that they become more fully engaged with their colleagues and with their building community. We believe many matters now handled as technical problems by administrators could be more productively handled by the full leadership team as issues of community policy. For example, a well developed school behavior code, along with conflict negotiation procedures drawn up by all members of the school community, could prevent the escalation of conflicts into full-blown legal problems.

Leaders of restructured schools must dedicate themselves over the course of their entire professional lives to development of increasingly complex, sophisticated values. Emphasis conventionally given to skills development must be shifted to values development. Skills, by and large, come relatively naturally as one's world view and frame of reference mature. Without moral maturation, skills by themselves are puny and inadequate. From their initial preparation, through induction-year training and into mid- and late-career growth, school leaders must be given the kinds

"Central office roles must change, too. The central office should become a resource/service center with people moving from traditional roles of director, controller, and monitor to enabler, facilitator, and helper."

of opportunities that promote the development of increasingly mature values.

Such values come not as received wisdom but as inner commitment developed through experience. Adults mature in this respect just as children do, by being given opportunities to make important choices (within but stretching the limits of their judgment and experience) and by reflecting (often with assistance from others more experienced) upon the results of their choices in ways likely to inform their future behavior. It is unfortunate that most professional training treats values as given and unchanging and skills as situational and dynamic. This emphasis must be reversed.

Training for restructuring leaders must expose them to the richest possible variety of school experiences, because they will need to be able to call upon a rich stock or repertoire of case situations and responses to be effective on the job.

Research on the development of expertise in such fields as chess, music, architecture, psychoanalysis, and teaching, along with many others, shows that it is based largely on the accumulation of stock situations and underlying situational principles that enable the expert to define a situation in such a way that especially effective action can be taken. We refer not so much to fixed experiences to be replicated over time, but to modal experiences that guide insight and judgment through changing circumstances.

It must be clear, finally, that formal training reaches only so far toward the needed preparation of skilled leaders. Every job experience is a training ground and every contact between professionals an opportunity for teaching and learning. Performance planning, supervisory evaluation, counseling and reviews, site visits, and the myriad other occasions that bring more- and less-experienced administrators together are important opportunities for professional development.

We need to engender increased discomfort and frustration with the existing system of preservice and inservice. By increasing the stakes, reducing opportunities for complacency, and amplifying openness and sharing, we can create strong and visible incentives for growth and development.

Much of what we have in place does not need to be scrapped. Most elements, however, will require substantial modification. There are fragments of these new processes in many districts and schools; but there are very few settings in which all of these elements are woven into an integrated and ongoing program of professional development, which prepares administrators to lead and sustain restructuring environments.

All Together Now ...

The magnitude of the design and development task requires that restructuring schools seek partners for designing and implementing a comprehensive system of ongoing professional development. Institutions of higher education, regional labs and R&D centers, professional associations, academies and centers, and the business community will need to

Performance planning, supervisory evaluation, counseling and reviews, site visits, and the myriad other occasions that bring more- and less-experienced administrators together are important opportunities for professional development.

develop collaborative relationships with school people as they design these professional development environments in the schools. Increasingly, the school and the district will become the setting for these learning communities, requiring that these resource institutions, organizations, and individuals work in the schools and within the context of the restructuring process itself.

Many have argued for a strengthened integration of preservice and inservice training. We agree and add that preservice preparation must be very different from what exists presently in most institutions of higher education. Training and preparation programs must assume a different model and vision of schooling and education. They must have a radically different view of the teaching/learning environment and of the way schools can be organized and managed to support that teaching/learning environment. The credentialing system may need to change as well. Some institutions of higher education have begun the revitalization of their administrator preparation programs. LEAD centers have such a revitalization as one of their primary agendas.

Preservice education must be very different from what exists in most institutions of higher education.

Because the worlds of education research and practice employ different reward and belief systems, it is often difficult to blend the interests of a higher education professor or researcher with those of the education practitioner. Work is needed to create connections and interdependencies between and among these levels and to develop ways of fostering collaborative research between university faculty and school practitioners.

One of the important responsibilities for the training providers is the transformation of the burgeoning knowledge base on school leadership. Unfortunately, transformation is typically conceived as the dissemination of better print products. Such static resources may not be sufficiently responsive to the requirements of this transformed training. Instead, training needs to employ video tapes, select seminars, action research, and other ways of capturing the dynamic work of restructuring leaders and restructuring teams.

The Limits of Training

Some potential and practicing administrators are just not appropriate for restructuring schools and no amount of education and training will make them so. Many of the skills and behaviors required of leaders of restructuring schools are either too costly to develop or unresponsive to traditional training. In many cases, selection might be a more productive approach to ensuring that leaders of restructuring schools have the required competencies. In some cases, consideration should be given to the selection process for these leaders and for creating teams of individuals within the schools, which collectively have all of the skills and knowledge required.

More attention needs to be given to matching individuals to school contexts. Administrators without the required competencies need to be helped to understand and accept the mismatches between the school's culture and their own beliefs and preferred behaviors. Where training, along with other appropriate measures, is not sufficient to create the needed match between administrators and their settings, we need to help them move to other educational settings or out of education.

Radically different schools need radically different leaders. It follows that the development and sustenance of these leaders will require a radically different conceptualization of preservice and inservice education and training. We need to move beyond training on isolated knowledge and skills to deep understandings and complex behaviors. We need to create learning environments in restructuring schools that support the development of appropriate behaviors. And we need to do it all collaboratively, tapping the knowledge, experience, energy, and commitment of all members of the school community.

Summary

The existing system of schooling is not adequately serving many of our children. Schools are failing to keep pace with the revolutions in learning and work taking place just outside their doors. As organizations, schools are failing their staff as well. Teachers' and administrators' entrepreneurial dispositions are stunted by "the system." Restructuring—reconfiguring the basic functions, operations, and organization of schools—may be the only appropriate response to the present needs and circumstances.

Review of the research and practice literature on restructuring schools revealed four elements of change that characterize these schools. It was found that restructuring schools reinvigorate programs and services for their children, expand roles and responsibilities for teachers and others in the school community, remove the rules and regularities that constrain innovation and improvement, and reconceptualize traditional accountability as internally directed quality assurance.

Based on an understanding of the distinguishing features of these restructuring schools, an amplified description of competencies and behaviors of administrators who initiate and sustain these schools should be developed. This description departs from the common taxonomies of leadership skills. It stresses, instead, **professional qualities** as well as skills and **leadership principles** as well as roles.

Professional qualities include those habits of mind and heart that enable restructuring leaders to concentrate their own and others' efforts on developing increasingly desirable and sophisticated values and outcomes. Such qualities enable them to work effectively within ambiguous and changing circumstances, to enable rather than mandate superior performance, to craft solutions to unique problems, and to imagine and bring others to believe in new futures for themselves, their schools, and their students. Such leaders of restructuring schools employ human resource management, organizational development, and systematically examined experience that enable them to create dissatisfactions, forge interdependencies, manage change, and encourage risk taking.

The [education and training] process should 1) integrate learning and work; 2) emphasize action-oriented, problem-solving approaches to training; 3) focus on the development of teams; and 4) be comprehensive, coherent, and continuous.

Effective leaders are guided by a clear sense of purpose and can inspire others to that purpose. They are able to discard unproductive ways while holding firm to their beliefs. Deep commitment to collaborative action and shared decision making motivates them. They are masters of pertinent curriculum content and pedagogy. They are able coaches and cheerleaders. They promote pervasive and effective communication. Courage, faith, and persistence help them through the uncertainty and resistance they encounter. They are helped to meet the challenges of change by openness, flexibility, and willingness to experiment. They have developed maturity through deep, thoughtfully examined experience. They have well-developed faculties of reflection and judgment.

Educating and training administrators in these qualities and competencies require changes in the syllabus, the setting, and the process of administrator education and training. The process should: 1) integrate learning and work; 2) emphasize action-oriented, problem-solving approaches to training; 3) focus on the development of teams; and 4) be comprehensive, coherent, and continuous. Restructuring schools must themselves become learning communities and serve as the primary sites for preparation and training, providing the essential environment for mentored, individual job-centered study. The structure of training should mirror a key value supporting restructuring schools; collaborative learning requires horizontal, web-like networks of professionals.

This redesign of administrator education and training for restructuring will require a collaborative effort between the schools and the several providers of preservice and inservice programs. These providers will need to work at the restructuring site, integrating training and support into the day-to-day work of administrators and administrator/teacher teams.

On the basis of our study, we find that

- The values, beliefs, and assumptions that drive restructuring schools are very different from those of traditional schools. The substantial differences in restructuring efforts promise to actually make a difference in learning for students and for all members of the school community.

- Leadership matters. As schools restructure to share decisionmaking authority and responsibility, new forms of leadership will be essential. Administrators will need to provide that leadership in partnership with teachers.

- Restructuring involves not just schools, but the larger school community of parents, community members, and business leaders.

In the spirit of the principle that form follows function, the essential elements of restructuring require new administrator competencies and behaviors.

- Educators need to be concerned with much more than training. We need to recreate schools as learning communities where all members— teachers and administrators, as well as students— grow in and through their work. We need to consider new settings and processes for preparing potential and practicing administrators.

- Education needs new professional development structures to support administrators working in restructuring districts and schools.

- Leadership development is a shared responsibility. Institutions of higher education, professional development academies, regional labs and centers, and the business sector must join with the schools in providing a coordinated and ongoing program of education and training.

Recommendations

Restructuring requires that schools, universities, policymakers, and all others engaged in the education enterprise adopt a revised conceptualization of leadership. Leadership must be appreciated as a capacity encompassing not only skills at wielding the tools of administration and management, but a combination of values, habits of mind and heart, and experience. It is the latter elements that define the ablest leaders, for their greatest challenges come in situations that transcend the limits of skills and their application.

Restructuring requires that schools be seen as learning communities. There are two important implications to this perspective. First, learning—true learning as opposed to rote mastery or test taking—requires a balanced regimen of stress and failure, elation, and success. Second, part of the business of school is to develop the school staff. Teachers and administrators do not come to the job perfectly formed, nor does their development follow a straight line. Only in the school constituted as a learning community will their professional growth continue to match the needs of their organization.

Restructuring requires that all the parties engaged in educational staff development—along with some that do not now participate—enter into new relationships with changed roles and responsibilities. Schools, as we have said, must change from factories to learning communities. Universities, school boards, associations, central offices, and communities also must change. They will have to set aside accustomed roles, enter new partnerships, and take on greater responsibilities. To this end, we suggest that:

Schools

- build education and training into their day-to-day work;

- create learning tasks that are linked to improvement priorities;

- establish opportunities for teachers to practice leadership behaviors; and

- identify teachers who have potential to serve as administrators in restructuring schools.

Districts and superintendents

- shift their mission from mandates and control to facilitation and technical assistance; redirect resources to support school staff;

- emphasize staff development and leadership supervision over performance evaluation; manage people, not procedures; appraise performance as a problem-solving and professional growth strategy;

- develop interlocking district and professional strategic plans; reward professional development that contributes to the school and district, as well as to the individual;

- espouse (through action) values of achievement and excellence in concert with change, risk taking, enablement, collaboration, communication, recognition, and reward; and

- create teams of central office and school staffs, community, and board members to work together on instructional leadership, restructuring, staff development, and other key issues.

School boards

- develop a clear sense of district purpose, and attach school improvement and professional development plans to it;

- adopt a plan for leadership recruitment, selection, and development that is consistent with district goals;

- acknowledge the importance of professional growth for administrators and teachers, and increase the district's investment in their professional development;

- find the restructuring schools in their district, learn how the things they are doing could be expanded to the entire district, and find ways of encouraging their efforts.

Providers of administrator education and training

- reconstitute the syllabus for training around the skills, dispositions, and behaviors that comprise the restructuring leader;

- de-emphasize attention to the traditional course structure of administrative preparation programs;

- design courses as sets of integrated and holistic competencies linked to restructuring tasks and activities;

- address the principles of adult learning and incorporate attention to policy implementation and institutional change;

- study administrators working in restructuring environments and, in order to design appropriate education and training programs, learn more about the circumstances and behaviors of administrators in these districts and schools;

- bring professional development resources to the school campus and to the routine practices of restructuring schools; and

- develop collaboratives for design and development, joining with administrators in restructuring districts and schools to identify essential competencies and the appropriate training content and processes.

State legislatures

- shift the emphasis on certification from credits and institutions to a combination of skills and professional qualities;

- treat leadership development as a priority deserving of state funding and technical assistance;

- work with the chief state school officer to shift the state department of education role from funding and control to enablement and facilitation; and

- create a critical mass of restructuring schools in their states and provide them with the resources needed to survive and succeed.

Restructuring schools do not create themselves. They require enlightened leadership for their initiation and sustenance. We must attend to leadership development if we are to realize the potential of restructuring for improving the education of our children. The barriers are many and substantial, but they are not insurmountable. Instead, they help us to appreciate the dimensions of the opportunity restructuring presents for students and for all members of the school community.

Appendix A: Study Group Members

National LEADership Network
Study Group on Restructuring Schools

Ms. Dianne Ashby
LEAD Director
Illinois Board of Education
100 North First Street
Springfield, IL 62777
(217) 782-5728

Ms. Mary Campbell
Coordinator
U.S. Department of Education
555 New Jersey Avenue, NW
Washington, DC 20208
(202) 219-2130

Dr. Kate Dickson
Director of Curriculum and
   Instruction
West Linn School District
West Linn, OR 97068
(503) 638-9869
   (Former Director, Oregon
   Leadership Academy)

Dr. Patricia Duttweiler
Senior Policy Associate
Southwest Educational
   Development Laboratory
211 East 7th Street
Austin, TX 78701
(512) 476-6861

Ms. Joy Kromer
LEAD Director
KanLEAD
820 Quincy - Suite 200
Topeka, KS 66612
(913) 232-6566

Dr. Patricia Krysinski
Assistant Professor
College of Education
Washington State University
Pullman, WA 99164
(509) 335-2530
   (Former Director, Washington
   LEAD Consortium)

Dr. Betty Lindsey
LEAD Director
Kentucky Academy for School
   Executives
1121 Louisville Road
Frankfort, KY 40601
(502) 223-2758

Dr. Richard McDonald
Co-Chair
Principal, Arongen Elementary
   School
Box 54-970, Route 146
Clifton Park NY 12065
(518) 371-8105
   (Former Director, New York
   State LEAD Center)

Dr. Charles Mojkowski
Co-Chair
LEAD Director
RI Educational Leadership
   Academy
78 Foxglove Drive
Cranston, RI 02920
(401) 944-3850

Ms. Sandra Orletsky
Director, School Governance
   and Administration
Appalachia Educational
   Laboratory
P.O. Box 1348
Charleston, WV 25325
(800) 624-9120

Dr. Laraine Roberts
LEAD Director
California School Leadership
   Academy
313 West Winton Avenue
Hayward, CA 94544
(415) 887-8808

Mr. Nelson Walls
LEAD Director
Maine Leadership Consortium
University of Maine System
150 Capitol Street
Augusta, ME 04330
(207) 623-2531

Elizabeth Hale
Vice President, IEL

Hunter Moorman
LEAD Program Manager

Co-Directors, National LEADership Network
Institute for Educational Leadership
1001 Connecticut Avenue, NW, Suite 310
Washington, DC 20036
(202) 822-8714

Appendix B: Select Seminar Participants

Select Seminar on Training Administrators for Restructuring Schools
September 30-October 2, 1989
Xerox International Center for Training and Management Development
Leesburg, Virginia

California

Laraine Roberts
LEAD Director
California School
    LeadershipAcademy
Hayward, CA 94544

Thomas Payzant
Superintendent
San Diego City Schools
San Diego, CA 92103

David Gordon
Deputy Superintendent
California Department of
    Education
Sacramento, CA 95814

Illinois

Dianne Ashby
LEAD Director
Illinois Board of Education
Springfield, IL 62777

Joseph Scime
Superintendent
Community District No. 300
Dundee, IL 60118

Yvonne Robinson
Principal
Gavin Elementary School
Chicago Heights, IL 60411

Kansas

Joy Kromer
LEAD Director
KanLEAD
Topeka, KS 66612

Max Heim
Superintendent
Junction City Public Schools
Junction City, KS 66441

Larry Dixon
Principal
Junction City High School
Junction City, KS 66441

Kentucky

Betty Lindsey
LEAD Director
Kentucky Academy for School
    Executives
Frankfort, KY 40601

Marilyn Hohmann
Principal
Fairdale High School
Fairdale, KY 40118

Charles Edwards
Principal
Woodlawn Elementary School
Danville, KY 40422

Maine

Nelson Walls
LEAD Director
Maine Leadership Consortium
Augusta, ME 04330

Constance Goldman
Superintendent
Gorham Public Schools
Gorham, ME 04038

Gary MacDonald
Principal
New Suncook School
Friburg, ME 04737

New York

Richard McDonald
Principal
Arongen Elementary School
Clifton Park, NY 12065
    (Former Director, New York
    State LEAD Center)

Edward McHale
Superintendent
Shenendehowa School District
Clifton Park, NY 12065

Marie Cianca
Special Education Supervisor
Charlotte Middle School
Rochester, NY 14612

Oregon

Wayne Robbins
Associate Executive Director
Confederation of Oregon
  School Administrators
Salem, OR 97301

Kate Dickson
Director of Curriculum and
  Instruction
West Linn School District
West Linn, OR 97068
  (Former Director, Oregon
  Leadership Academy)

James Ford
Principal
Sheldon High School
Eugene, OR 97401

Rhode Island

Charles Mojkowski
LEAD Director
RI Educational Leadership
  Academy
Cranston, RI 02920

Salvatore Augeri
Superintendent
Westerly Public Schools
Westerly, RI 02891

John Thompson
Staff Development Coordinator
Westerly Public Schools
Westerly, RI 02891

Washington

Patricia Krysinski
Assistant Professor
College of Education
Washington State University
Pullman, WA 99164
  (Former Director, Washington
  LEAD Consortium)

Vivian Murray
Executive Director 6-12
Bellevue School District
Bellevue, WA 98009

Jill Matthies
Principal
Newport Heights Elementary
  School
Bellevue, WA 93006

Regional Educational Laboratories

Patricia Duttweiler
Senior Policy Associate
Southwest Educational
  Development Laboratory
Austin, TX 78701

Sandra Orletsky
Director, School Governance
  and Administration
Appalachia Educational
  Laboratory
Charleston, WV 25325

U.S. Department of Education Office of Educational Research and Improvement

Mary Campbell
Study Group Coordinator
Programs for the Improvement
  of Practice
U.S. Department of Education
Washington, DC 20208

Appendix C: Description of Study Group Activities

The Study Group on Restructuring Schools was formed at the November 1988 meeting of the LEAD Directors-National LEADership Network in Washington, D.C. Initially, the group examined the broad topic of restructuring education but quickly came to focus on the special challenges involved in providing professional services to help principals and other administrators initiate and sustain restructuring efforts.

The work plan was divided into three phases: study and reflection, discussion with practitioners involved in restructuring, and dissemination and implementation. During Phase I, Study Group members reviewed the extensive literature and developed a comprehensive framework for examining restructuring efforts. On April 16-18, 1989, the Study Group met at the JCPS/Gheens Professional Development Academy in Louisville, Kentucky, to share information and talk with expert consultants and practitioners regarding their experiences and observations about restructuring.

The meeting featured presentations by Dr. Phillip Schlechty, President, Center for Leadership in School Reform, as well as a superintendent, two high school principals, a central office staff person, and members of the Gheens Academy staff. Presenters also made themselves available for open discussion and exchange of ideas with the group. Members had the opportunity to learn from reading they had done before the meeting (bibliographies and copies of articles were provided) and from presenters, other local administrators who were invited to lunch and dinner, and from each other. These activities formed the basis for Phase II, a more intensive conversation with practitioners.

To add depth to our analysis, the Study Group conducted a "select seminar" from September 30 through October 2, 1989, at the Xerox Training Center in Leesburg, Virginia. Each of the nine LEAD Directors invited two administrators (a superintendent or central office administrator and a principal) who were involved in restructuring efforts in their states, to discuss the changing roles, competencies, and training needs of administrators. The select seminar, a process used frequently in the New York State LEAD Program, allowed this group of educators the opportunity to engage in reflective discussion and writing based on their craft knowledge and experience.

The goal of the seminar was to consider the issue of training administrators for restructuring schools in terms of the changing roles and needs. The essence of the seminar was its attempt to bring the complex issue of restructuring back to where it belongs—to those most affected by it. The select seminar provided an opportunity for a group of seasoned education leaders with a wide range of school-restructuring experiences to make a statement to their colleagues, particularly to those who design and deliver training for school administrators.

The seminar process encouraged reflective and creative thinking. Throughout the 3 days, small group sessions focused on tasks related to the three major questions that guided the seminar (as noted in the Introduction). Participants worked on these tasks in role-alike and mixed groups. They had many opportunities for reflective writing and rich discussion, and the notebooks in which they recorded their observations during the seminar were turned in to the planning team at the conclusion of the session. Much of the material in this report was taken from those notebooks.

The seminar followed a very simple structure based upon a set of guiding principles:

1. Participants need to commit adequate time—to study, to work, to reflect, and to write.

In preparation for the seminar, participants spent a 3-month period of intense study and review of the literature on restructuring. The planning committee screened and distributed the literature, making certain that each participant reviewed readings and research that addressed the full spectrum of restructuring. The seminar was conducted over 3 days —September 30 through October 2, 1989—at the Xerox International Center for Training and Management Development in Leesburg, Virginia.

2. A conducive work environment is very important.

The Xerox Center provided a "protected environment" away from the work site and in aesthetically pleasing surroundings; extra care was given to the quality of food and refreshments. We believe this was an important step in communicating to participants both the special nature of the seminar and the high expectations that their deliberations would have important results.

3. The seminar participants are the experts.

We believe that the select seminar process is successful because of the high degree of personal and professional respect afforded participants. These individuals represented years of educational experience and training; they constituted the body of experts. While participants did extensive reading from the work of outside experts in preparation for the seminar, visiting experts and lecturers were not a part of the seminar process.

4. Roles are "checked at the door."

This seminar included school superintendents, principals, administrators, LEAD directors, and Department of Education personnel. But ideas stood on their own; they were debated, accepted, or discarded without regard to the participant's position, prior experience, or education.

5. Select seminars are self-governing entities with organizers serving the group.

The coordination of the seminar was managed by the planning team which, after providing the initial structure and ongoing logistical support, transferred governance and direction to the participants. It is fair to say that, by the end of the seminar, it was self-governed and coordinators were taking direction from the seminar group.

6. The experience is as important as the product.

Seminar participants agreed that the process—the experience—is most important. This report provides documentation of that experience and of the participants' efforts.

ED/OERI91–5